SANTA'S CHRISTMAS
TOMTENS JUL

A Swedish Christmas counting book

En tomte
One Santa

1

Två stugor
Two cottages

2

Tre älgar
Three moose

3

Fyra julgranar
Four Christmas trees

4

Fem adventsljusstakar
Five advent candlesticks

5

Sex slädar
Six sleighs

6

Sju julbockar
Seven yule goats

7

Åtta snöglober
Eight snow globes

8

Nio snöflingor
Nine snowflakes

9

Tio julstrumpor
Ten Christmas stockings

10

Elva snögubbar
Eleven snowmen

11

Tolv pepparkaksgubbar
Twelve gingerbread men

12

Tretton
lucior
Thirteen
lucias

13

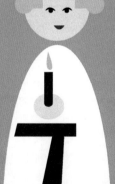

Fjorton lussekatter
Fourteen saffron buns

14

Femton julklappar
Fifteen Christmas presents

15

1

2

3

4

5

6

7

8

9

10

11

12

13

14

15

Tomtemor
(Tomte mum)
Mrs Claus

Tomtefar (Tomte dad)
Santa Claus/Father Christmas

More Christmas Words Fler julord

Julafton Christmas Eve

God Jul Merry Christmas

Julskinka Christmas ham

Julgröt Christmas porridge

Grötslev Porridge ladle

Pepparkakshus Gingerbread house

Önskelista Wish list

Julkort Christmas card

Julsånger Christmas carols

Adventskalender Advent calendar

Stjärngosse Star boy

Hejsan! [Hello!]

Hi, I'm Linda. I'm a Swedish mum living among the rolling green hills of Surrey in the United Kingdom together with my Dutch husband, bouncy toddler, and boisterous Swiss dog. As you can tell we're an international bunch, and we speak English at home.

I write bilingual children's books to share my native language and some Swedish culture with our young bookworm whose first language is English. I hope your little explorers will enjoy the books too while growing their Swedish vocabulary.

If you've enjoyed this book, please consider leaving an honest review where you bought it, as it will help other parents find and choose it too.

Id'd love to stay in touch. You can find me on Instagram and Pinterest (@linda_liebrand). Join my newsletter at www.swenglish.life and get a free bilingual book!

Want More Swedish Books?

My first book about Sweden – Min första bok om Sverige
From lingonberries to Falu red cottages and Vikings, this picture book introduces Swedish traditions, culture and everyday fun. Both kids and adults will love the gorgeous colour photos.

Counting Sweden - Räkna med Sverige
One Midsummer pole, two Vikings or three crowns? Just imagine how many typically Swedish things there are to count. Kids will have fun counting from one to ten while learning to recognise some of Sweden's most loved national symbols and traditions.

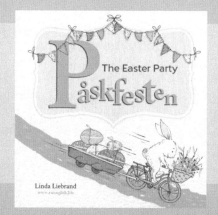

The Easter Party – Påskfesten
A fun Easter story for kids aged 3-6. At the end of the book, they'll learn more about Easter eggs, Easter witches, Easter twigs and other typically Swedish Easter traditions.

First Printing 2018
Treetop Media Ltd
www.tree-top.media

Made in United States
Orlando, FL
23 November 2024

54319664R00020